THIRTY DAYS' NOTICE

Cath Kenneally lives in Adelaide and is a radio
producer and broadcaster and arts writer as well
as a writer of novels and poems. Her collection
Around Here won the John Bray National Poetry
Prize at the Adelaide Festival of Arts in 2002.

By the same author

Harmers Haven

Around Here

All Day All Night

Ci Vediamo

Room Temperature

Jetty Road

Angela Valamanesh: About Being Here

Acknowledgement

Many of the poems in this book have been previously published
or broadcast, including by *Southerly*, *Heat*, *Jacket*, *La Traductiere*,
Big Weather (Wellington), *Famous Reporter*, Writers Radio, Poetica,
Iron Lace, *Best Australian Poems 2007*, *Jacket 2* and *Atlantic Review*.
Some have been translated into Lithuanian and Romanian.

thirty days' notice

cath kenneally

Wakefield
Press

Wakefield Press
1 The Parade West
Kent Town
South Australia 5067
www.wakefieldpress.com.au

First published 2012

Cover design by Liz Nicholson, designBITE
Typeset by Wakefield Press
Printed and bound by Hyde Park Press, Adelaide

National Library of Australia Cataloguing-in-Publication entry

Author: Kenneally, Catherine.
Title: Thirty days' notice / Cath Kenneally.
ISBN: 978 1 74305 103 0 (pbk.).
Dewey Number: A821.3

Government
of South Australia

Arts SA

fox creek
wines

Contents

on your mark

Pola sneezes ... another bout of 'kennel cough'?
The bamboo, pampered since the depredations of
a hired hand sent by the visitor who gushed
over our 'sacred grove', begged 'a little' for
his Japanese *ryokan* in the hills,
looks well, this autumn morning

I ogle the postcard of the Wylie Baths
regarding me from my windowsill
and wish myself there. Will it always
be the case that a perfect day here
only prompts yearning for
the glorious yonder?

A shield, the university crest
under my nose – they write to whip
me to the finish, get my thesis in
today – the printers – then my ruined hair
chlorine pools, alas, not Wylie's
pause for pecan bread – new favourite

a tour of the garden while eating
inspect baby aloes and echeverias
removed from under parents' wings,
replanted round the side, haphazardly
dotted about the neglected yard
which calls to me piteously

so far so good – all this is bluff
outfoxing my demons, burbling-spring
technique, one mustn't pause – quick:
last night's dream – blended-families flick
a round-table, Richard Grayson mooting
'Death and Dying' as an Artists' Week theme

at my elbow, one boxy gym slip, 'Girls College Wear
The Myer Emporium (S.A.) Ltd.', $2.75 yesterday
from the Salvos warehouse, mid-calf, never worn
space on the tag under Myer's name, for yours
'olive drab' is perhaps the shade – too bright for 'khaki'
a garment from my school vintage

60s, from the zip-pocket's metal teeth to the telltale
'Emporium', thin, elongated Roman script
on the elegant tag, letters embroidered, not printed;
poignant, now, the care that went into detail;
from the yoke fall graceless pleats, beneath which
all but the beauties struggled to shine

Today's college-girl wears pleated kilts
and shorts for gym. Friday morning Phys Ed
for us was bread-and-butter ball games
till Bernard, the science nun, blew in
like a twister, waving rust canvas bloomers and
daffodil shirts, for hurdles, the long jump, shot put

and discus – muscles were in, shorts out.
Those gathered panties
far naughtier, Spartan boudoir wear.
Marie the boarder, Hugh Grant forelock
flapping glamorous on her forehead
ran like Diana, bloomers sculpted to her bum

frank thighs pumping, golden skin and eyes like
the sky over the wheat fields she came from
she cleaned up that new-style sports day
save the marathon and walking-race, won by
the girl with the biggest chest, speed-lurching
in a jolting catwalk, vibrato breasts transfixing
the boys' school drum band.

Most days I pass that sports field
the school now mixed, boys' cricket whites
dotting the green like seagulls
I wonder where the girls' team is
where fleetfoot Marie got to

as I dress for work
I ponder parallel bruise-lines
running down one thigh, like
nothing so much as cane-marks
not a clue how they got there
my boys observe me from their photo

looking out from an Islington pub
the front room of The Angelica
Stacey side-on, her sunny smile,
her friends Joely, and Clare and Robi
I lift a benedictory pint to them
hoping they are in the pink, as Mum would have said

make a tough-guy move with one hand
flick the palm a few times towards my face
come on, Monday, let's have ya

charge nurse

depth-charge migraine
aftershock bouncing side to side in brain-pan
Pola knows this is no ordinary lie-down
I hear her clip up the passage
into the room
stop beside me
to lick my fingers
where they dangle
from under the covers

she trips softly away
returning every five minutes
to perform the same ceremony

I'm cheered, beneath the pain
and touched. How have I earned
              this devotion?

ambush

Head floating in mid-air, an aura surrounds
you as you step, new-minted, into the garden, where
greens ambush you, sharp, citric nibs of Geraldton Wax,
spearlets, yellower green, of bamboo, comforting
blue-green of gum leaves, dark moss-green creeper
fronds, tough all-purpose bougainvillea green
there's a sense that everyone's gone to the moon
as in the old song, and you may be imagining
the stillness, but no, everything's poised,
on its mark, holding its collective breath
your skull feels the size of a beach-ball, similarly
weightless, any moment you'll slip your moorings
ascend into the welcoming branches of this
blue-gum, join the silent throng of swallows

cypress of lebanon

only mournful palms and cypresses
in the Brethren front garden
for ages there was nothing
eventually a sticking-plaster lawn
then the palms went in, and now
two cypresses, ramrod-straight
guard the drive, saluting the white
wagons sailing in and out

blooms may be too frivolous, immodest
only men and boys made the garden
do the plants have to be from the Bible?
The psalms mention 'cypress of Lebanon'
and there's Our Lord's palm-strewn progress
into Jerusalem. These two are spindly,
fronds parched and yellowed.
Two little girls have appeared on the lawn

perky, bright-coloured dresses, rebuking
my prejudice, no doubt the back yard's
crowded with swings and slippery-dips
There's a new Brethren house one street over
with no front yard, just a low wall
but maybe a wilderness of flowers
out the back, what do I know?
A friend whose flat overlooks

a Brethren yard in Goodwood
says the lawn comes alive on Thursdays
when adults meet inside while shrieking
delighted kids run riot into the night
Not a Lebanese nose among them, but.

dressed in yella

My voice-reading facility kicks in
as I listen to the recording
with forensic precision it deciphers
her answering-machine message

one part frightened, two parts breathless
My sister sounds harried, almost asthmatic
and that's her work voice
Oh dear. I'm too far away

and powerless in any case
still in the grip of
eldest-sister
God-complex

I put on my pink satin slippers
switch to Cinderella. Pola stops by
to lick my chin. She doesn't
need saving

ghost gums

Two hunks of lawn hoed up
for a ghost and a gimlet gum
Good luck, fellas, we'll keep
the turf out of your toes
possums out of your hair
with these wire cages and tin trims
Since the flats behind us axed the blue gum
that shaded us as well, we're naked
to afternoon sun

At the native plant sale at the Showgrounds
we've found in addition an *albapurpurea*
a red mallee and a 'plunkett',
all billed as hardy; they'll need to be –
no Peter Cundalls here. This week
Pete was in Hobart at a church garden working-bee
grubbing out sycamores and limp hydrangeas
plumbago ('out it goes!'), whacking in
azaleas and gardenias

The priest seemed depressed
underwhelmed by God's good earth
Acacia floribundia, white sallow wattle
to clothe the naked boundary fence
a startling shade called merino
stridently new, replacing ivy-choked palings
The wattle leaves are round at first
then taper out to spears. Full sun
to dappled shade

Hard not to do sums as you plant.
In ten years' time, twenty, who'll
be standing by this honey-myrtle?
We've found old photos of the yard
twenty years back, new-laid
The jacarandas in the street
spindly and thin, towering over us now
as we bend back towards the earth
Look at Pete, though, going on eighty,

lunging in muck up to his armpits
– You know what I'm about to tell yer,
I'm not planning on checking out yet

but when you do, where better to end up
than the compost heap?

freestyle

best of the day is the swim
late afternoon sun slicking
the skin of the *plein air* council pool
glowing true-blue after its refit
new edges flush with the ground
so the swimmer's eye meets water
dreamily continuous with land
a shoreline giving way to grass
one unbroken, glossy plane

I choose the relaxation lane
although the slow one is free
for its greater elbow-room
and a certain pressure, also
is brought to bear on lane-
swimmers to keep up.
Often the slows appear to
be trying to prove they're
fasts on a rest-break

Alpha Blondy sings roots
reggae for me when I return
I like his hymns most
'Come Back Jesus' and 'Jeru-
salem, Here I Am', triggering
buried responses I don't bother
to block, cant-catcher
gloves hanging slack
at my side

I vow to fix the portable Olivetti,
sea-blue enamel, that sits
on the bookcase, so pretty
so 60s, so Barbara-Pym-
in-a-bedsit, or someone
more glamorous – Elizabeth Jane
Howard, wasp-waisted gorgeous,
beset by cads, marrying the
brother instead of the beloved

then the egregious Kingsley
fun at first but not for long
hanging in through thick & thicker
shickered & shickereder. She's
written her story, alarmingly
kind to her husbands – she kept
choosing wronguns – an unloved child,
a spirited woman of substance and style
who'd adore the housecoat

I've thrown on post-shower,
great clumps of freestyle
tangerine chrysanths, plopped
on a green-blue ground
amid lime-yellow leaves,
slashed lapels and fitted bodice
tightly-cinched waist, long
ribbon belt to tie in sassy bows
and a fifties fandango froth

of unfettered skirts

Donnybrook

they've closed the streets
for Dagwood Bumstead
United States Defence Chief
doing lunch with Downer
a plebiscite of vehicles
assembles tamely
behind the barriers

all change

Oaklands Station, stuccoed shelter walls, insides finished by pressing
thin-fluted galv-iron against the render, a strongly claustrophobic effect
all painted Zambezi-sludge ochre, as if the stop had once been swamped
under a jungle flood, and left to dry

thought has gone into achieving such stupefying dreariness
unmatched at other stops along the line, Ascot Park washed gay sky-blue
Woodlands top-of-the-milk cream, our own Clarence Park dotted with
miniature roses in jade cement wells

the Oaklands stationmaster has carefully chalked up today's train times
on a child's blackboard alongside his window, perhaps only to discourage
importunate passengers, perhaps out of love of the job,
white for all stops, pink for express

I've been to see baby Bella, my nephew's newborn, at their flat right opposite
alongside the tracks, paddocks such as studded the suburbs when we were
    kids
houses demolished a decade back, except for kerbs, leaving open land
soon to be Marion Swimming Centre

Bella's softball head fits neatly in my cupped palm
She rests in the crook of my knee, dreams like a kitten,
startles, mews, eyelids taut, tensing and slackening
her legs and arms

    She may learn to swim in that new pool, unless her mum and dad
    go to teach in the country, a plan that sounds cosy, old-fashioned, safe

As I wait on the station for the train home, Leah walks by beyond the fenc
in a green and white striped hoodie, pushing a catafalque pram,
hunched over her baby as they make for their one-up one-down, studiedly
   nondescript, sandy brick, cunningly angled to get no sun at all

back at my place, the back lawn's sea of green is gaudy
the orange tree's crowding globes flamboyant
mid-May sun pinking my neck and gold-
dusting the yard, brashly munificent

     I teleport Nicky, Leah and Bella into a sunny yard in a beach town
     Robe, say, halfway up a wide street lined with jacarandas

like the single mum's place in The Caterpillar Wish,
that I saw last week, old, timber-frame, not too glossy,
instantly lovable, peeling wallpaper, fading paint
light gushing in from all sides, sea tang

in the brisk autumn air, so that the girl in the movie
always wears a llama-wool hat with earflaps
and a cherry-red duffel-coat as she rides her bicycle

generous footpaths for cycling and running,
walking and dawdling, a house with a Mr Curly front gate,
broad steps to the verandah, wide front windows,
enough rooms to get lost in, the way they built homes
'in the day', as Nick would say, sunroom screen door banging softly

     an old trike with rubber pedals sits waiting
     under the Moreton Bay out the front

               Go, I think, go now, go

a little rain

The hot spell broke last night
Today, light showers, not even enough
to damp down the sandy dust in the front yard

But just the sight of rain slanting earthwards
seen from under a café awning, lifts the spirits, germinates
resolutions: baking, planting, travelling

I bake pecan bread, cosset the rebel oven
the loaves look fine. Bougainvillea scales the front wall
making a saffron backdrop for birds, a shrill type – wattle?

We continue with Schuyler's letters, having finished Padgett's
Life of Joe Brainard. To Joe, Jimmy writes: 'So in England
weight is still given in "stones" ... So the English are much more

stoned than we ... Some day Uncle Wiggily will tell you all about
rods and poods, though it may not be for a score of years.'
Smashing to get a letter from Wiggily – or any letter

one with a stamp, and someone's witticisms, not gonna happen.
A long-stay guest at Great Spruce Head Island, Schuyler
hung out for 'the mailboat' – more romantic still

A baroque concert this afternoon, very Jim, and home to French paperbac
another of his loves, stacked in the kitchen, saved from Georgie's toss-pile
Duras, Hugo, George Sand, from her French course, Newcastle, in the 80s

Les grands marées, Un barrage contre le pacifique
two watery titles. On the Duras cover, a painting, tidal flats and grasses
grey low water. *'L'année suivante, la petite partie des barrages*

qui avait tenue s'était à son tour écroulée.' Jim's last year to the letter.
Odd one out in the stack is *Herb Gardening*, Clare Loewenfeld. 'Sometimes
lemon balm shoots up very early in spring, if there is a warm spell'

There was! It did!

isle of oblivion

Packing for the island
towels, to leave there
Sorbolene, cosmetics samples
in tiny bottles, to leave
crime novels, ditto
Deny King, King of the Wilderness,
In Tasmania,
The Wollemi Pine,
Duras' *'barrage contre le Pacifique'*
not much use against
the Southern Ocean

Dreamt of a name for the house
saw myself standing outside it,
under a sign
it's gone again

The thesis is packed in a shopping trolley
to be carted to the Graduate Centre
and deposited this morning

I long to be rid of it, but it'll leave a hole
What to worry about now?

My eye skids sideways to the guidelines
at my elbow. 'The Critical Essay
as a general rule ...'
too late

take this
writing pad
mobile
postcards
library books
magazines
CDs
brain-wipes

hotfoot

and so to Bruny: the house could be 'Bruny Doon'
as in Bonnie Doon (from The Castle; remember
'We're going to Bonnie Doon, we're going ...')
or not

Eh, eh, ah, ah, chortles a crow in perfect Italian
shallow sleep last night, letting in crowd dreams
the whole neighbourhood hotfooting it to our place
to see some celebrity who'd been installed here
a posse of Italian women, *nonna* out in front
racing down the street, pushing a table on wheels,
showing the younger, fuller-figured *donne*
a clean pair of heels

what shoes to take? My trusty Humans, black suede
pleasantly louche, skater shoes, really, bought
with Bek and Tom in Melbourne before I went to Paris
- thongs, slippers – must call Tom, who I fear is downhearted
and who Annie says is moving to the country, to Castlemaine
Bek's folks' place, where they were married outdoors
a hot December 3rd, two years ago.

London crime novels in, and Eating Up Italy
Voyages on a Vespa, a ripoff of Peter Moore's Vroom
with a View, from which I copy a list of gelati flavours
cioccolato, nocciola, croccantino, stracciatello,
zuppa inglese, cioccoriso, caffè, nutella, dolcelatte,
fiordilatte, pistacchio, spagnola, melone, cassata

frutti di bosco, fragola, banana, limone, ananas
latte di mandorla. I'm there. Pizzo, Calabria,
a hole-in-the-wall family-run icecream kiosk
isn't *fior di latte* a cheese? Like *bocconcini?*
I've just written to a Milanese *pensione* for Don,
at work, using my rusting Italian. '*Colazione*'
was a reach, an index of how *rapidamente*
it's vanishing

The Jetstar flight is late. Di, meeting me
will be cooling her heels
at the airport

antropy

A thorn in the pad of my left index finger
swells it like a plump cherry tomato
probing reveals the tiniest sliver of slick brown
which must be impressively toxic, like the ants
Jack Jumpers, the most venomous on Earth

Native to the Island, aggressive,
they take the fight right up to you. Allergic
folk have to move elsewhere, when the next
bite could be their last, a scant two minutes
to grab the antidote

runway

At the shack next door, the son
has it in for the banksias, cuts down
two grown trees in his one day there
Mum moping on the back porch

They've already scraped their sloping block
bald, scoured a runway to the beach
those banksias were growing peaceably
on our edge of the creek

perhaps they blocked the water-view
from her deck-chair, positioned
at the very edge of the verandah
the viewing seat must be nailed there

Our blackwoods are thriving
blue gum saplings and others
one or two old fellas newly slumped
across the creek

Mudhens, partridges, a gang of blue-
winged parrots bathe communally
in the wide pond midway down the flow
prettier than rosellas, chartreuse breasts

splodged with teal. The wedgie who
patrols the sheep paddock hasn't shown
Come back, bring your friends
use the landing-strip next door

Simpsons Bay gatepost

Peace Haven
Trespassers Prosecuted
Dogs will be Shot
No Shooting
All Prior Permission
Is Forthwith Withdrawn

Crying Girl

brisk-trotting down the bike path
propelling Junior in the pram, keeping close up
against her bloke who's striding it out, steely-jawed

I thought you'd be there, she bawls, loudly, way
past caring that this walker who's drawn level
might eavesdrop. Her late-teens tight-packed fleshy

face is blotched and smeared. She dashes snot and
tears across it with one hand loosed momentarily
from the buggy handle. They belt ahead too fast

for me to hear his answer, save that it's dis-
missive, curt, and I can see he looks straight
ahead, rotating a rollie between his fingers

he won't be there, that seems clear, perhaps just not
today, perhaps not for the wedding, or christening, or
    never again.
He's a cartoon tough, stays rawhide dry while she dissolves

She's leaking at all the seams but he's a fish's bum
they're coming unstitched by the waters of Tamar
the holey family of Launceston

detail

Melbourne buzzes and fizzes when the sun shines
sol rather than *sal volatile* added to a beaker of hoomins
In the Gallery, pudgy children lead their fathers where they will
straight under Leonard French's ceiling, to the pretty lights they go
A sign at my elbow reproduces Durer's triumphal arch
for Maximilian 1, never built, commissioned solely as a print
so crowded with detail it overwhelms the eye

In the plaza, below, an arch of sorts, blue plastic plinths,
two outsize angular dumbbells. We've gone off
fine detail. A woman with very short hair passes beneath me,
another, jaunty in a hat, strides ahead of a happy detail of men
we would once have called retarded, no more
unkind than 'disabled' – kinder, in holding out the hope
of catching up

The Impressionists

for Ros

He looked the same, till I noticed
the welts on his arms, eczema curdling
the skin on his legs, below long shorts.
He'd come to collect their younger girl, same
pixie features above narrow ribs, now mooring
figurehead breasts. He used to dote on his
first-born, who's backed off, fingers burned,
too many cancelled appointments, as he
navigates new waters. The house seemed less warm
than last time, unloved, part of the floor
pulled up, awaiting a finish, living room
unlived-in. But she has her market produce
spilling over benches, as ever, packing
away as we speak, sorting old herbs from new
by feel, storing some and binning others
fondly patting Jerusalem artichokes into place
in a cupboard, slapping meat on a board
to precook for a rendang next day, her kitchen
humming: We talk about travels, and time remaining.
Her house is where I situate a precise moment
when I felt most as though I had all the time
in the world, all things were possible, life
for the taking – the weekend I caught the bus
from Adelaide to see The Impressionists
at the National Gallery, thirty-two, cheerfully

blind to someone's rival notion my life
was for their taking, soon to be acted on.
She always seemed to grab hers with both hands
clutches it firmly still – my spirits rise as I
watch her chopping oyster blade, top grade
proclaiming her stalwart carnivorousness
Let us be anything but bloodless, I think
smirking at her kitchen-wall poster, two
women shoppers at a market stall, holding
up fruit for inspection, one telling the other
'The grenades are in the lemons'

Airwick

The smell of your own house,
that you don't notice unless
you've been away, but others do

can't be reproduced, is different
to anyone else's, and others
will remember it as your family smell

as you remember the houses
of childhood friends – the Billingtons'
somehow compound of brains

which you were never served
anywhere else, the rosewood casing of
their piano, and the sour-sweet

tang of Mrs B's genteel distress
at her dashing husband's womanising
plus some buttery element

and the boy smell of Mary's brothers
absent from the Somervilles' newer,
larger home in an airy beach suburb

where Gloria baked pavlovas
and judged her daughter's friends
by whether they rinsed the sink

after washing up. That house was
Mister Sheen, Gloria's hairspray
her new carpets, Mary-Jane's Tweed

on velvet dresses in her walk-in robe
her one sister neatly stowed in a
separate bedroom with no smell at all

while Anne-Therese lived
in just as swank a house, vibrant
as the Somervilles' was mute

with earthy elements of dye in Lebanese rugs
and Mother's spices thickening the air
traces of grilled meat and honeycakes

Our place had a wet-laundry smell
with notes of boot polish and
boiling mince, a lingering presence

of beer-dregs in the sink, a history
of fried lamb chops and a bathroom
tang of dire fake-lemon shampoo

that stripped your hair of shine
Dad's Palmolive shaving-stick soap
and my Bonne Bell skin-toning lotion

as used by Libby, in her Beaumont
bedroom, her older mother always home
placing pot-pourris and flowers, not

quite masking an aged smell of used
vigour, stale talc, Yardley Lily of the
Valley, the fusty forties fanning

from the felt front of
their open radiogram

landline

In the Botanic Gardens I meet Evette Sunset, squirrel-eyes in pecan face
plaiting banana palm slivers she'd stripped from boles like giant leeks
she looked to have struck root there, veins coursing with sap, a naiad,
a tree nymph; I, with my microphone, clodhopping, dense.
Forest, whisper my true name, unfurl braids down my back
press my palms to the earth, find me a landline

Cracks in the Cloister

was a book of cartoons
aimed at clerics, monks and nuns -
'In the world' says a nun with a face
like Boris Yeltsin 'they used
to call me Little Funpot'

Who said, 'the world
is too much with us'?
when you shut the door
behind you at close of day
brochures litter the table

bills beg from their basket
newspapers blot the sofa
but the phone is silent
low-slung autumn rays
traverse dusty windows

the world's suspended
playing dead. In five minutes
the quiet turns oppressive
You go outside, on the pretext
of bringing in washing

really to hear the sounds
from next door: Peg
romping rowdily with
her grandkids. Returning
to the house, you leave the door open.

Maleficent

Push back to the surface
   from under a slab   of Chiltern rock,

   Peak District gritstone
         heavy as shame

A bad fairy wants the man of my dreams
   who's tall, chemo-bald, thin as a rail
      but coming good
         Oh, my heart

We meet in a hall opening out onto pillows of downs
bustled by crowds, our hug, after years, warm and strong

He lives by the sea,
   on a road umbrella'd
      by kind trees
         the strand pocked with warm pools

He stretches his lean length in one, still dressed

      his cool sunroom has a daybed under louvres
        looking out to the beach

   Bad Fairy goes to bathe and make a meal
      I sit on the couch, his long legs at my back
         yearning and dread thickening the air

Bad Fairy's food is mounded
      in wells in a white dish

poisonous pellets of fish eggs
a curdled mousse of squid ink
jellied kelp in slivers

Her damp hair twists around her face
into black foam
She will be sans merci,
our struggle to the death

Kindergarten of the Air

Home alone in the afternoons, I put on kids' TV
for the illusion that nothing changes – Thomas the Tank
and Playschool. I see my toddler self skipping
to these same tunes, on Kindergarten of the Air
when presenters sounded like the Queen
In the seventies, Playschool was all Anglo
John, John, Noni, Bettina – maybe Bettina wasn't
By now they've had every kind of host but Sikh
yet they stick with English nursery rhymes – Jack and Jill,
Miss Muffet, Mother Hubbard still standards, if deliciously
skewed when sung by a bouncy Japanese girl
and a gay Greek man called Theo

milk glass

Twenty years ago milk was out – 'mucus-forming' – now its mode
of production is suspect, we avoid it for fear of breast cancer,
or buy organic and cross our fingers

Moi's boys, my cousins, would stand after footy at the fridge door
downing pint upon pint, glass empties lining up on the bench,
six left daily on their doorstep, as on ours

Till I was ten, our fathers shared a milkround; we approved of milk,
souping-up sickly warm playground half-pints with flavour-infused
    straws
blissfully chemical chocolate or strawberry

Later, school-milk came in tetra-paks, silver-lined hexagons
    designed to
erupt when you bit off a corner; no more bottle-necks to collect
    cream
tinfoil tops disappeared from the earth

then school milk vanished too, going the way of inkwells,
    ringworms, jungle-
gyms and marching-in. Dad taught us how to wash milk-bottles –
    rinse first
in cold water, then hot suds, then cold again

I'm standing with him
at the Sturt Road kitchen sink
whenever I wash a milk glass

nest

In the queue ahead of Anna and me
beefy, shaven-headed young bloke
slumps over his trolley as he waits
tiny Thai girlfriend propped against him
When it's their turn, they unload
a rugged denim jacket with fur collar
onto the checkout counter, some WD40
metal paint in a black can
a second Big-Man's jacket in indigo
then a size 8 pair of white tracks for her
and one set of three nesting rattan baskets

disco man

flat and heavy, a disc like the ancients used to fling
Dad's tape-measure was the antithesis of electronica
brass winding-tap for belly-button, toothy steel buckle
drawing the cloth tape from its brass-lipped mouth,
hand-painted black and red numerals and gradations
marking parchment-coloured fabric, all embursed
in tan leather and weighing several pounds
it lived in the back of his Hills Hoists panel-van
in daily use for measuring the length and breadth
of fences-to-be in the new suburbs to the south
to wield it was to claim kinship with
a fortunate band of draughtsmen
assayers of firm foundations
augurers of permanence

mud lotus

Goldie Hawn's *Lotus Grows in the Mud*
for review, Hollinghurst's *The Line of Beauty*
for reading-group – beauty's tracery spelt out in a cover-shot
of flowing double-curves
curlicues on grand house-gates
beyond, blurry hedges, perspective retracting
to a pillar of far-off light, entry
to the moated grange, the private park, the lake ...
'a love of the world that was shockingly
unconditional' is thrust upon Nick
expensive knowlings amassed
by boys and men reduced to
tokens in elaborate games
multi-layered sensibilities honed
at toney colleges, street cred, business
nous, endless nuances
down the toilet in the end
Goldie's big on faith, but you have to go with doomed young Nick
gobsmacked by 'the fact of a street corner at all'
staggered by the being-there of wind and stones
twigs   rubbish   leaves   grass   rain

Jenny's hideaway

daphne on the windowsill, in the bow
      window of Jen's new studio
a stun-gun jolt of aroma

rollercoasts me back to the terrace
      outside the nuns' recreation-room
where I spy briefly on Sister Rockjaw, bent

over her prize bush, features softening
      as she whispers to it
A Wellington electric bus slides by

bisecting the opposite hill, tethered
      to overhead wires by two poles that give it
the character of a fast-moving snail

antennae flung back as it breasts a head-wind
      clouds march double-time across the horizon
behind a regiment of peaks, the daily

invading army sweeping over Hataitai alps
      holding formation as they press on
I rehearse the paper I'm to give tomorrow

extolling fictions for older women
      decrying the failings of chick lit
a late-bloomer crying for company

cerise oleander thrives by the cage out there
        I take to be for rabbits (in fact for hedgehogs,
a staging-post before they go back on the road)

those poisonous mid-winter blooms invite an
        easy segue, which I reject in favour
of claiming sisterhood with the gardenia

still fragrant, but dropping the odd blossom
        on the desk, from a miniature urn Greg seems
to have painted repeatedly, and fellowship too

– clichéd but on-the-money – with the forget-me-nots
    in the blue cup, while not demanding attention
thickly flowered, modestly insistent

Red Wellingtons

Red Wellington boots
not Paddington-Bear wellies
but bought in Wellington, Diesel brand
cherry-red, very Flash Gordon
a squashed D embroidered on each toe
just as comfortable as gumboots
reminding me as I pull them on
of Soup, the shop they were bought from
in Jenny's company, the same day as
a Marilyn Sainty skirt, blue,
and lined with shot silk

Soup an up-market secondhand-designer place
next door to the real thing, whose name I forget
the toffier one on the ground floor, with Soup
downstairs in a century-old cellar in reclaimed
warehouses at the docks, brisk wind off the water,
walls a metre thick, painted quiet cream
in the expensive shop, shrill bargain white
in Soup, which is crammed with clothes
where the other has a decorous few
with pretty handmade labels that burn
your hand. It was my last morning,
a trip nude of shopping so far
the boots and skirt acting as
confirmation I'd been there
and of the superior choice

Wellingtonian women
have, fashion-wise

the night before, I wore old clothes
to a curry-house, where we argued
the composition of certain rocks
with Elizabeth and Fergus
and I drank lassi. Jen
wore her green wool jacket
chic, unfussy, clean-cut
straight hair parted on the side
a forties look, almost severe
Elizabeth had stepped straight out
of Persuasion, brown ringlets and round
specs on the end of her nose
a lace shawl, the plump cheeks
of an eternal eighteen-year-old
writing fantasy does that for you

Jen dropped me at the airport
on a windy rooftop we hugged goodbye
boots and skirt in a rough-stamped paper bag
to show their high-class provenance
Ten years since my last visit
these are homing boots, I say
like the red shoes
minus the pain
see you in
the spring

surrogate

Today, walking home to Linda's
down Bland Street, I meet a woman
in a fawn felt hat coming the other way, who

halts and throws up her hands as she draws near
shakes her head and smiles: 'Oh! I thought you were
my daughter who walks towards me!'

Her hands trace my silhouette in the air
'Same shape.' I smile back. 'Same, eh?'

'Same hair.' She indicates my spikes,
smiles more broadly, and we both shake our heads
'Ah, well,' she says, moving off, 'all the best.'

'Wait,' I want to say, 'tell me more
about your girl.' Let me bask a minute longer
in surrogate daughterhood

By the time I reach Number 77
I have a new mother. She is
Hungarian, fled the Communists in '56

I was born here in Sydney after she arrived
My name is Celeste

Island Queen

The bus is for thinking, thinking, or pretending to. I find I'm thinking,
wow, driver, you're burling along.   Burling?

Jen's poem's open on my lap about the sadness of a father's death
which turns itself into a boy's illness that ultimately declares its origins
like a path uncovered in digging up the garden

a wonderful cyclical poem that takes half an hour to read
as long as the bus ride, with gazing out of the window at the flying houses

She lives in a men's house, sole woman among four, who once preferred
boys to girls: 'that's changed, though I still envy them their shirts'
Yes, I try to wear men's shirts, but they don't sit well

I envy small-chested women, Jen being one

Burling, burling through the back streets home
The Rocky Shore is what she's called her poem,   witty, wandering,
'I don't want to repeat myself but I do', she says, repeatedly

Jen's oldest, apart from stepson Jack, Felix, now walks ahead of her and
    Carlo to school, won't be seen keeping company with his mum and kid bro
She never thought that would happen but it has

Felix still lets her kiss him goodbye

Once when my eldest was five, his teacher left him behind in the Botanical
    Gardens, after an excursion, collecting the others, ferried them back to
    school in the bus

My mother, arriving to collect him, discovered the oversight

drove back to the Gardens and found him, a boy among trees
I will never know what he was thinking, my lay equivalent of the moment
Gerard Windsor notes, waiting while his son made his First Confession

I think of Yuri in London surrounded by a forest of buildings

a boy among glass trees, though provided now with a bicycle
to make his own way home along Regent Canal, burling along,
thinking, maybe, of his mother thinking of him

Skirting the rocky shore as Jen's mob do, going with the flow
making landfall safely, for a waterside beer
in the Island Queen

note: 'The Rocky Shore': title poem of Jenny Bornholdt's
2009 VUP collection

revenu

in the photo, baby props himself
on mother's chest in the bath
her hair in a striped towel
gazes unsmiling into her eyes
which beam back at him

that's how he is, thoughtful, benign
at home with man and beast
enters the chooks' conversation
as he crawls around the garden
in their company

he likes all people, drunks in the park
derros in post-office queues
an old soul, the world
recognises him
welcome back

staples

rice flour sago rice
flour sago sago rice
sago flour rice rice
the kitchen's blaring
four-letter words

from cream tin canisters
badged amidships with decals
squat blue tubs of red geraniums
on a red-and-white frilled sill
to a chorus of tea, tea

tea, tea, tea, tea, tea
I have two sets, one with red lids
one with green, but the red-lids
are short a big brother, flour
you need more flour

than sugar, rice, or tea
or sago. The sets stopped
including sago in the 60s,
surely. These cream tins
are the same as Mum had

when she married, I suppose
a wedding present, likely
I can see them ranged on the
green mantelpiece over the
wood-stove alcove

bookended with an electric clock
cream and black. When we moved
they came along, joined later
in the seventies by a plastic set
fire-engine red, white lids

no sago, coffee now, and
tea, sugar, flour, rice
or not rice, something else?
hardly cornflakes, or bran
or milk powder or matches

baby formula, cornmeal,
soap flakes, chilli
oats, macaroni – nope
semolina we had, but that
didn't make the series

plastic or tin. The plastic
too is now collectible
I have some, not on display
My green-lid tins were ten
bucks each, but came

with Mum thrown in
she did cook us sago
for a while, but it fell
off the menu when
4-Square began

to carry ricecream, Deb
instant mashed, frozen peas
packet soups. In a share-house
the kitchen had bins
built under benches

we felt obliged to fill
with flour, sugar, and
what else? – rice
the rats must have got some
we cooked a lot of bread

Mum kept dripping in a bowl
till Dad discovered safflower oil
the plastic canisters displaced
the tins. Their lids didn't sit
as tightly. Their labels read

from top to bottom. Tin-lids, us
kids, dropped and cracked them
My green-lid cream tins sit high up
only Flour filled, and Sugar
my other staples pantried

in glass jars, or the packs
they came in, clamped
with pegs and rubber bands
the teas, though, fill a bench
living in bakelite, older again

cream with red lids
cream with blue
all-cream but mottled,
I need them all – green tea
camomile, linden, peppermint

Twinings fruit allsorts, Dilmah
Tea's still for comfort
flour – gluey stamina
sugar for get up and go
rice to march on

Sago – what? to fill any gaps
like polystyrene beads
in bean bags we'd yet to meet
Did it have any food-value?
a patriotic intake –

Eat Commonwealth. We did.
Our tea Amgoorie, white-turbanned
sikh on dark-skinned paper
CSR sugar farmed by Kanaks
far from their island home

flour from close at hand
wheat fields to our north
Laucke and Fowlers Lion
who still guards the roof
of the old factory

now an arts hub
across from Central Station
I have the small spices set
of course, cream and green
and cream and red

cinnamon nutmeg cloves
pepper ginger mace allspice
above their innocent heads
a hold more florid
than a Spanish galleon's

Mum reached for cinnamon, nutmeg
never cardamom, coriander
pods and husks 4-Square knew not
cumin and turmeric I buy in bulk
always forget what I've put in

the ginger canister, or the pepper
salt relegated to a small dispenser
I surround myself with echo-
chambers, while my sugar's destined
for cakes from Morocco, Portugal

flour's for flatbreads made with
buttermilk and scallions
the pantry store is flush with
drygoods linking me to the world
not just Empire

Though I don't imagine they're
produced by happy freeholders
I think of them in kitchens
in Jedda, in Lisbon,
Tripoli and Salvador

Of bush tucker, there's a jar
or three, Anna and I buy them
each year at the still-Royal Show
relish and chutneys – Raj-inspired
made from wattleseed, quandongs

lemon myrtle, bush pepper, tokens
of uneasy goodwill, kept cupboarded.
Flanked by cream cylinders
I set about cooking
they send me cheerios

this is the Hospital Hour – my
pianola brain emitting sub-aural
hum: sounds from the middle
of last century: B–I–N–G–O
and Bingo was his name, oh

she's the sweetest little rosebud
that Texas ever grew
Mum didn't fit the mould
how many did? Sometimes it seems
the mould's got tighter

Sometimes I float in air too thin
to drink. Can't say my cans
are prayer-wheels, but I touch them
over and over, for luck
Just for luck

praxis

discover
purpose
in the
wisdom of
a chest
bug

oxygen-
starved
brain
simply
wants
you
to
sleep

can't
be arsed
noting
violent
red
of banksia
searing
lime
of planes

except
as possible

sources
of your
misery

    make
    no
    decisions
    don't
    take
    stock
    sleep
    is good

        practise
        sleep

at a pinch

'She moved like a woman twice her age'
a woman twice mine would make the
Guinness Book of Records for just being there
but I'm moving like her today
a mean vertebra pinching a nerve

while the wind whines outside
saving me the trouble
and rain begins to tap out a tattoo
on the roof, skies darkening
from one second to the next

Our Christmas tree looms darkly
in a corner of the lounge room
dirty patches on the white sofa cover
show up startlingly well in the gloom
Pola lolls on the newly washed armchair

a ladder leans against the pergola
inviting cat-burglars to try their luck
as the only human in the house
I consider the rats and the possums
mice and cockroaches

lizards and spiders
who never think about cleaning
though they consider this house home
They have chosen the better part
Let them keep an eye on it

while I hobble out for coffee

small hail

I talk to my aunt on the phone. She says
a cousin's eldest, just out of nappies
for her PhD on women in Chile
    made a film about Michele Bachelet
        in the year of her presidential run
    while living with rural families
          out of Santiago. Our girls
are superchicks: Anna outlines
        this country's constitutional quirks
      piloting with cool aplomb her blue Charade,
weaving us in and out of tight spots
        before they can get beyond close-fitting
I make a mental note to brush up my manual driving
      at least I can admire her agility and acknowledge my
        rustiness
          at the same time
I cheer them all on from the sidelines
        but always check the forecast:
      Small hail, the man says.
        don't hurt so much as the golf balls
    but harder to dodge, eh, Zeke?
        Let's hope the big hail never comes
          clattering on the tiles
But they say the Chileans chafe under a woman's hand
      Ségolène, in France, is disliked by women
        this throaty French voice on So Frenchy, So Chic
        seems a threatening purr:

I'm way - ting, I'm way - ting,

j'attends

j'attends

Erin go bragh

Looking up, I lock eyes
with my grandmother, Ellen
glowing in her frame, full lips
held slightly apart in the middle
– as if she's just blown a kiss –
with the faintest of smiles

a frank gaze from under
untutored eyebrows
head and shoulders shot
hair parted left, softly caught back
fluffy at the sides, uncoiffed
lit gently from the right

a weighty cross on a thick-linked chain
at her throat, unwieldy insignia
what seemed a soft collar now appears
as maybe a hood thrown back,
the single-button garment as
a cloak or loose summer coat

of muslin, all white, maybe
a Children of Mary cape
She's very young, perhaps eighteen
childish contours cover the
familiar bones, repeated now
through three generations

She keeps her counsel
is this a coming-of-age shot
one taken for her fiancé
or the end of school
or her Confirmation?
She might be only sixteen

– of the Faith, anyway,
first and most important
She's leaning forward into the
future, as if dragged down
by the heavy crucifix

I see her mother hanging it
round her neck, a label
an amulet, a compass

pick a number

Thirty-one thousand: the cost of this house
in 1981. Seventy-five – the one
around the corner, two years later

The family's first phone number:
seven double-six five oh two
the cousins': nine six two five double two

Street numbers of houses you've lived in
except for Sydney ones, which didn't imprint
75, 354, 19, 13, 46

the years you made trips overseas
the price of a kilo of mince in '75
(a dollar). How much it cost

to get into the pictures, up until
you were ten (sixpence, ninepence, a shilling)
your mother's age at the birth of her last child

– 43. How many runs your father made at the SCG
in 1951 (12). The size he took in shoes (10)
how much you weighed at sixteen

(eight and a half stone). The year you left school
but not the years your kids did. The dates of
deaths in the family – but you need to work backwards

from these to figure the birth-years of mother,
father and brother. You know your divorced sisters'
old phone numbers, not their new ones

can never recall what happened three days back
but know the sums you asked the operator
when phones had Button A and Button B:

How many holes in a crumpet?
How many bubbles in a Coke?

clearances

They're on their way, in ones and twos,
across the continent, between hemispheres
to this dot at the bottom of a dogleg peninsula,
where I wait, making room at the inn,
beds, three, four, five, I could do ten
dried food and fresh, clean sheets
and hot water, each space an embrace
aired and sweet, lawns green and plants watered,
new gums stretching leaftips in mute how-do,
Sunday Market to stand in for Sunday Mass,
new local pub a step south, a wedding for year's end,
new blood to old, a gathering of the clan
and then the clearances, tenants out, laird
and lady rattling round the empty
keep

A Doctor Calls

Kookaburras in the gum tree, mother and fledgling
Junior's cute in that standard baby way, blunt of beak,
chubby where the olds are lean, fluff instead of feathers
ma and pa are hooked, they chaperone, they watch her diet

Buses rumble in the next street, one of which is mine
but I'm waiting for this call, bathers in my lap
reminding me to stop for a swim on my way home
from work, where my schedule is loose

the thought of that ride to town, half an hour or so,
makes me squirm; some days I achieve absence, travel
in a brown study, but not today. Christmas is coming
our plan to ignore it dispelled by our chick's return

from her trial flight. We'll have a tree, do Farmers' Market,
aim for jollity, short of a Christmas truce with the bad guys
My baby, storm-pummelled, limps home from the tropics
to hole up in her redecked nest, red and black like an

Oriental hotel, with white touches for mourning.
A daily ale at the Avoca is a plan, while food,
yours, mine and ours, resumes centre stage – *à propos*,
The Doctor calls – I try for kookaburra cheer

Hear, Hear

Soft, chiding wail floats over
the fence: the baby remonstrating
more in sorrow than anger
comforting itself with gentle tears
today's sun too soft to sustain anguish
the dog gets off the couch to investigate
responding to distress-signals, but the sobs cease
and she trots back in, takes a different chair
apart from that, no sound impinges

Yoga teachers instruct you to close off
your hearing, starting with distant sounds
progressing to nearer ones: hard to do
you settle on a far-off car horn, say,
then the closer rumble of a train,
bells at the level-crossing, birdsong
in trees outside the Institute windows
the person beside you breathing
at first, sounds mingle and blend

the state of carlessness has sharpened my ears
I pick the brrr of the bus mooching gently by
a street away. Back on my bike after decades,
peg the warning growl of cars grumbling up behind
a motor-bike coughs its three-stage rev
and powers past. I dreamt today of a moped
being sold by two bottle-blond London lads,
480 Euros, square and safe, low to the ground,
I was handing them the cash when I woke

There goes a council truck
grinding through gears
a crow ark-arks, someone is
hauling a rattling trailer
another hoons round the corner
on two wheels, just for the heck of it
heavy slam of a four-wheel-drive door –
that'll be Greg, Greg and Amy
with the new baby

Gabe and Stacey go in for
Hopi ear-candling –
thin, hollow wax tapers
introduced into each ear
then lit, acting as syphons
that funnel stiff grunge

alluring to think one
might draw old poison
lodged even deeper

imagine a cleared auditorium
where never is heard a
discouraging word
and the lies are
unshrouded – hooray.

An Air (after Haydn)

Papa John Paul's dead and gone
No to condoms still his song
When the world's awash with pus
We'll know that's his gift to us

holy war

At early tables, scattered cups
the usual breakfasts for a smaller crowd
spurts of traffic pass us by, with intervals
of quiet while the lights are red
baby-buggies fewer on a holiday weekend
babes-in-arms seem strangely still
clouds overhead coagulate, ruched swags
of darker-grey over grey-white shams

Talk is of bombs and plots, devilish agendas
unholy grabs across the globe for oil
deep under halls of unkinged mountains
as millions step into appointed places
a mammoth Ziegfield Follies, the hippie trail
restocked with seekers in tanks and turbans
their freedom fight ordained
but not by Allah or the God of Hosts

unless we've got it wrong. Our godless eyes
don't see the giant fist raised high
above the clouds, clenched tight
around the bolt prepared forever
for a race of evildoers
sipping final cappuccinos

breakfast of champions

the taste of holiness
filled the back of your throat
as you listened to the stories

bracing, tannic overtones
of blood and iron, of
creek water running off

peaty soil, brown yet
clear right down to
the sandy bottom

Vincent, Thérèse, Martin,
Anthony, taking it on the
chin, downing their doses

slights and slaps, jolts
and jabs, the beef tea
of the soul

some siphoned off to
prime the lifelines
of the hungry ghosts

swallow, said the Bishop
to the Foundress – Mary
of the mud-brown Joeys

black billy-tea with gum-
leaves, twirled round her
head, swilled from the

tin mug of obloquy
all that dun-coloured troop
you could salute

but never love -
lepers beneath their cloaks
phthisic babes belted

to their backs
dull-witted scholars
ranged at their feet

you danced out of range
of the call-up, drab
fatigues, wintry struggle

strained instead towards
the distant hum of
a demon bike

whose rider had your name
tattooed on his arm
in spikes of vermilion

blobs of lustrous black
curlicues and flourishes
of sulphur-green

spider, man

In London this summer the spiders are swarming
as Earth warms up like an Aga
thuggish Indian ladybirds, bigger and tougher
are ousting the sweet English girlies
They'll have to find something else
for the spines of kids' storybooks
Australian spiders continue to thrive
but our birds are hard-pressed, crows

tweaking fruit through hairnets on trees
in good times they stick to carrion
Obscurely worried, we walk fretful dogs
by moonlight, beneath jacarandas frothing
with the usual blueburst, passing
the usual huddle of cars, dragon-breath

quenched for the night; they rouse in us
as yet, only a mounting peevishness

if, on a winter's night

In the back of a handbook of home
remedies I find a pencilled query:
Whatever happened to Dave Healey?
Memory kicks in on a winter night
two figures in matching trench coats
on Somerton Beach, holding hands
under a black sky
the dark esplanade lamplit at intervals
gently buffeted by rain and spray

running away from a dismal soiree
at Pam's who had a thing for musicals
uncool to the max: 'South Pacific' on
her Kreisler stereo, she strumming
a cheapo guitar she couldn't play
murdering the tunes, singing half
a note flat,
We, fainting with ennui, made tracks
Weewanda Street wound to the beach

At Sacred Heart, Dave was
A second-go matriculant, fair, quiet,
knowledgeable, funny, older than my fifteen
He'd have been waiting for a sign
some secret thumb-press that I'd
have liked to know, because
I liked him
that look of puzzled, fond forbearance
Hello, Dave. How was your life?

Wakefield Press is an independent publishing and
distribution company based in Adelaide, South Australia.
We love good stories and publish beautiful books.
To see our full range of books, please visit our website at
www.wakefieldpress.com.au
where all titles are available for purchase.